# GAME ANIMALS
## OF
## NORTH AMERICA

# GAME ANIMALS
## OF
## NORTH AMERICA

Text and Photographs by

## J. DAVID TAYLOR

Crescent Books

Copyright © 1988 Discovery Books

This 1988 edition published by Crescent Books, distributed by Crown Publishers, Inc., 225 Park Avenue South, New York, N.Y. 10003.

ISBN: 0-517-65712-0

Library of Congress Cataloging-in-Publication Data

Taylor, Dave.
    Game animals of North America/text and photographs
    by Dave Taylor
    p.      cm.
    Includes index.
    ISBN 0-517-65712-0.
    1.  Game and game-birds — North
America.    2.  Mammals — North America.
    I. Title.
    QL715.T38 1988
    599.73'097—dc19                                    87-36511
                                                        CIP

Printed and bound in Italy

h g f e d c b a

# CONTENTS

INTRODUCTION   7

1   BEARS   10

2   THE YEAR OF THE DEER   34

3   ANTLERED BIG GAME   62

4   HORNED GAME   84

5   SMALL GAME: PREDATORS AND PREY   108

PHOTO INDEX   144

# INTRODUCTION

A cougar cub soaks up the summer sun. Cougars are
shy, solitary creatures that hunt nocturnally.

FOR YEARS NOW I HAVE PURSUED THE GAME ANIMALS OF NORTH America with a camera. It is an interest that has its roots in the days when, as a teenager, I hunted rabbits and dreamed of the day when I'd stalk grizzly and elk.

When that day came I'd put aside my shotgun and rifle and replaced them with 35mm cameras and telephoto lenses. There were many reasons for this change but perhaps the most important was my growing interest in the animals as living creatures rather than as a source of food or trophies. Over the years I've photographed many other species not considered game animals but this group has remained my preference.

The term game animals refers to those animals sought after by hunters. Under its broad umbrella come waterfowl, upland game birds and a variety of mammals. *Game Animals of North America* limits itself to the mammals of North America which are traditionally considered to be game animals. These include bear, deer, bison, muskox, sheep and goats, small game (such as rabbits and groundhogs) and some predators. They do not include seals, whales, bats, most furbearers and small rodents, or birds. Each chapter looks at a different aspect of the life and history of these animals.

Nowhere in the world does a wildlife photographer have the freedom to pursue so many species of wild animal as here in North America. The national, state and provincial parks provide a tremendous range of habitat and species and can be visited by anyone who wishes to see first-hand the wonders of this land. Outside such preserves are even greater opportunities for wilderness adventures that expand the potential of the photographer.

I hope that, in this book, I have been able to share the wonder I have felt for the beauty of these magnificent animals.

The coyote is one of the most successful mammals on the continent
— its range has expanded substantially in the twentieth century
despite man's intense pressure to exterminate it.

# BEARS

Polar bears are excellent stalkers. In order to remain inconspicuous as they approach their prey, they may even slide forward on their bellies.

NORTH AMERICA IS HOME TO THREE SPECIES OF BEAR: THE BLACK bear, the grizzly and the polar bear. The most common and widespread of the three is the black bear. It is found in forty-three of the fifty American states from Florida to Alaska, and in nine of the ten provinces and both territories of Canada. Only the central plains states and Hawaii, and the province of Prince Edward Island lack the species. Black bears are the smallest of the North American bears, weighing on average between 200 and 600 pounds. Contrary to what one might think, not all black bears are black. It is the most common color in the east but in the western states and provinces, brown and cinnamon black bears predominate. On an island off the coast of British Columbia there is even a white subspecies known as Kermode's black bear, and on the southern tip of the Alaska panhandle there roams a "blue" bear known as the glacier bear.

Grizzly bears were once thought to have several subspecies but today are divided into only two: the grizzly or brown bear and the Kodiak bear. The two subspecies come in many color phases, ranging from black to brown and even blond. They can be distinguished from black bears by their grizzled coats, an effect created by their white-tipped fur. They also have a massive shoulder hump which the black bear lacks.

A grizzly's weight depends on where it lives and what it eats. Bears living on the tundra of the far north will average between 200 and 600 pounds while the coastal bears will weigh between 400 and 1000 pounds because of a rich diet of salmon. Kodiak bears, found only on Kodiak Island off the coastline of Alaska, can weigh up to 1700 pounds!

Once grizzlies ranged over most of North America from Labrador to Alaska south to the great plains and California. Today there are less than 500 south of the Canadian border, and these are confined to the northern American Rockies. There are no longer any found east of Hudson Bay in either the United States or Canada but they are still found in healthy numbers in British Columbia, Alberta, the Canadian territories and Alaska. Alaska probably has more grizzlies than all other areas combined.

Scientists theorize that both the grizzly and the black bear once shared a common ancestor. As the animals evolved, one species took to living in the forests and the other to more open country. This led to different patterns of behavior.

The black bear is a forest species. It relies on the forest for protection and, given the chance, will choose to slip into the cover of the woods rather than confront an enemy. Female black bears regularly shoo cubs up a tree if something dangerous is encountered or when leaving them to feed.

Because of this behavior pattern, black bears are seldom encountered in the wild even by experienced researchers with radio tracking equipment. When they are seen, it is usually at a bait or at dumps. The amazing thing about black bears is how tolerant they are of people under such circumstances. At dumps, children have been placed beside adult bears and ignored. One bear, surrounded by picture-taking tourists, staged a mock charge, scattering the people and securing a moment's peace before the bemused spectators returned to start the game again. The bear could easily have caught them but chose not to.

It is still well to remember that there are always a number of hostile encounters between man and bear. They average about one per summer throughout North America. Never take a bear for granted.

The grizzly on the other hand is a much more dangerous animal. Having elected to live in the open, it developed different behavior patterns in response to danger. Unable to slip away into the forest, the grizzly stands its ground and is much more apt to charge if it feels it cannot retreat. This behavior, while often bluff, is usually effective in causing the threat to move off.

At least this was the case until the Europeans arrived with their powerful rifles. Because of its stand and fight mentality the grizzly of the open country quickly succumbed to the settler's rifle. Once common in many great plains states and the southern portion of the Canadian prairies it is now extinct there. Even the mountain populations suffered until in the continental United States only remnant populations remain. In Canada the grizzly population is stable and it may even be expanding eastward into the Northwest Territories. Alaska's grizzly is not threatened.

The grizzly underwent certain physical changes as it evolved on the open prairie and tundra. Massive shoulder muscles developed to allow it to dig in the hard-packed earth in search of groundsquirrels. This knot of muscle gives the bear the characteristic hump for which it is known. Its claws, no longer needed for climbing, are suited for digging and are much straighter than a black bear's. It is a myth, however, that a grizzly can't climb a tree. It is true that they can't scamper up a tree like a black bear but they can climb any tree a man can if the tree isn't small enough to be knocked over by the irate animal.

Fortunately, few people will see a grizzly, even on trips to remote backcountry. New management techniques are being applied to reroute hiking trails away from prime bear feeding areas such as mountain slopes and berry patches. When a bear is known to be in an area it is usually closed until the animal leaves. In this way, perhaps the grizzly and man will be able to coexist peacefully.

The third native species is the polar bear, found along the arctic coast of North America. It is almost pure white although its summer coat may often bleach to yellow. Once endangered, it has made a heartening comeback and its numbers are steadily increasing. It is a large bear, weighing 800 to 1400 pounds on average. Like all bears, the female of the species is smaller than the male and, like other bear species, cubs are born in the den and will stay with their mother two or three years before she mates again. There are most frequently two cubs in a litter, although three are not unknown. Scientists now think that this bear is a white grizzly, or at least evolved from grizzly ancestors in the recent past. They do appear to be quite similar in silhouette, having the same body shape and hump. Like the grizzly, they are very aggressive for they evolved on the polar ice packs where there are few places to hide.

Unlike the other North American bears whose diet consists of eighty percent vegetation, polar bears are the most carnivorous bears on earth. Some of them, especially the males, may never eat any plant material. Females, when they come ashore to den, will eat plants but prefer a diet of seals, walrus, waterfowl eggs and other carnivore foods.

Polar bears spend most of their time on the polar ice cap hunting prey. Male polar bears do not hibernate and will seek a den only during the worst arctic winter storms. Females will den to give birth but for a much shorter time than the bears to the south. The availability of prey, expecially seals, year round is believed to alleviate the need for hibernation.

Food motivates a bear, any bear, anywhere. Hibernating black and grizzly bears do so because of the scarcity of food during the winter months. As omnivores they may eat more plant material than meat and so with the end of the growing season are deprived of food reserves. To counter this they spend the summer months and early fall feeding on whatever is most nourishing, gaining from a third to half their hibernation weight. For example, one large brown bear in late August weighed about 800 pounds, by October it topped 1100 pounds.

Hibernating bears are easily aroused because, unlike other hibernators, their metabolism does not slow down radically. Even so, very little of their fat reserves are burned up in the sleeping months but are saved for those critical few weeks between awakening and the first nourishing green shoots of spring.

Bears, like people, have very poor digestive systems. They need to find the most nourishing food available. For grizzly and black bears the best food is usually budding plants. They contain the most nutrients at this early stage and as the growing season advances they become less nutritious.

Grasses and sedges are among the very first plants to appear in the spring and for this reason bears are often found where these plants grow. In the Rocky Mountains south-facing slopes are favorite bear habitat in spring. Grizzlies will follow the melting snow up the mountain during the summer, feeding on each new fresh patch of vegetation. Black bears, however, restrict their feeding to open forest meadows and streams, seldom chancing the open mountain tundra. As the grasses mature and lose nutrition, bears turn their attention to berries, favored for their high sugar content.

Although omnivores, bears are still efficient predators and meat is eaten whenever possible. Recent studies have shown that black bears in Newfoundland and grizzlies in Alaska are significant predators on caribou calves. In the western states both species compete for the young of moose, elk and deer.

Dumps attract bears because they provide a source of highly nutritious food. Humans cook their meals to make food easier to digest and that appeals to bears' stomachs, too. Garbage dumps that do not thoroughly burn refuse are merely providing the bear with more digestible food.

Most parks warn that to "feed a bear is to kill it." Bears that learn that human beings are a source of better food than nature provides are smart enough to take advantage of it. In the past this led to bear jams in Yellowstone National Park. It also led to an increasing number of confrontations between bears and people. Finally all feeding of animals was banned for the safety of both man and animal. Bears that persisted in begging were usually shot.

Polar bears because of their high arctic range were free of this temptation almost everywhere but one place: Churchill, Manitoba. Here bears gather each fall to await the arrival of winter freeze-up when they can once again leave the tundra to hunt seals. Churchill happened to be built at their staging area and the town dump provided the bears with a delicious alternative to late fall sedges. As a result bears and people were constantly bumping into each other, sometimes fatally. Nowhere else in the world is it necessary for Halloween trick-or-treaters to be accompanied by armed bear patrollers. For the most part however Churchill's bear story is a happy one. A major bear-viewing industry has grown up here in the fall and both people and bears have benefited.

Although it is true that all three species of bear have killed and even fed upon humans, this is a rarity. The odds against being a victim of such an attack are less, much less, than being hurt in a car accident in your own neighborhood. Most hikers in bear country seldom even see a bear, let alone get close enough to one to be in any real danger. That is not to say that certain precautions should not be taken while in bear country. Bears are intelligent, powerful animals quite capable of doing a lot of damage if confronted or threatened. They are also, because of their intelligence, highly unpredictable animals and each must be treated as an individual.

Hikers and campers in bear country should keep food well away from their camps, suspended high in trees where possible. Garbage should be burned or packed out so that bears are not drawn to campsites after a group has left. A bear's nose is so sensitive that it can smell garbage buried beneath two feet of earth. Once a bear learns that campsites are good places to get food it will begin to visit them regularly, leading sooner or later to man-bear contact. Perfumed soaps and lotions may attract bears and should be avoided as well.

Making noise while walking is a good idea for it does alert bears that you are coming. It does have minor drawbacks, however. Bears that have never encountered people before may be drawn to the noise out of curiosity. Cubs especially are apt to do this. Some parks, notably Yosemite National Park in California, have occasionally developed bears known as "mugger" bears. These bears have learned that people mean food. They have also learned that by charging people they can cause hikers to drop their food packs when fleeing. Such bears are usually removed to remote locations by rangers or, if necessary, killed. In really remote areas, a bear may be very hungry or threatened, and attack. In general, however, it is wise to let bears know you are about, especially when there is bear sign in the area or if you are approaching favored bear habitat such as a berry patch or other food source.

Should you meet a bear closer than you'd like the best advice is to stand your ground and talk soothingly to it. Back off slowly facing the animal at all times. If it charges, do not run. Running invites it to chase and it becomes a game of tag that only the bear can win. Most charges are bluffs and end with the bear coming to an abrupt stop or veering into the woods. In the case of a real attack, lie down on your stomach in the fetal position with your hands behind your neck and play dead. Any resistance invites further attack, for the bear is trying to remove a threat and as long as you move the threat exists in the bear's mind.

If the bear seems intent on dining on you, it will usually move forward in a slow, deliberate manner. In these rare cases, running into a lake, climbing a tree or racing for a car are very good options. Failing these, the best advice is to charge the bear. Surprisingly this works, and works well, but only as a last resort.

The trend in recent years has been for man to try to understand the bear and its behavior patterns, so that we may learn to live beside this magnificent creature instead of having to destroy it. As a result the polar bear population is growing worldwide. The outlook for black bears is equally good. Sadly, the grizzly south of Canada may yet lose its battle. Yellowstone's population, one of the major aggregations of American continental grizzlies, appears to be losing more animals each year than are born into the population. Conservationists believe that with a better understanding of the bear's needs this trend could be reversed. A better understanding could also reduce the number of fatal confrontations between man and bear. Certainly the bear family is one of the most treasured of North America's game animals, and one worth saving for future generations.

Not all black bears are black. The spectacular cinnamon bear is not uncommon in the west.

Kermode's black bear is actually white or blond, and is found only along the coast of British Columbia.

A black bear of the common black color phase, lounges in the branches of a tree.

A grizzly cub overturns a rock, searching for grubs.

Grizzly bears are recognized by their dish-faced profiles and massive shoulder humps.

In this series of photographs, a grizzly catches and feasts on a
salmon that has completed its spawning run.

Although the smallest of the North American bear species, the black bear is still an imposing creature.

Bears stand to gain a better view or scent. They do not charge from this stance.

The most aggressive bears are actually cubs like these.

Once endangered, the polar bear has made a strong comeback in recent years.

Black bears weigh between 200 and 600 pounds. Even the largest of the species, such as this one, remain close to the safety of the forest.

Adult male polar bears may spend their entire lives on the arctic
ice packs.

The polar bear is now believed to have evolved from the same ancestor as the grizzly.

Above: Bears, despite their bulk, are remarkably agile and can run at speeds up to thirty-five miles per hour.

Right: A grizzly in Denali National Park stands, alert to any danger.

A black bear cub perches awkwardly in a dead tree. Cubs are often shooed up trees by their protective mothers if danger is near.

A grizzly bear ambles in the shallows of a river.

Two groggy grizzlies lounge in the sun after hibernation.

# THE YEAR OF THE DEER

The whitetail deer is North America's most popular
game animal for hunters and photographers alike.

THERE ARE TWO SPECIES OF DEER FOUND ON THE NORTH AMERICAN continent: the mule deer and the whitetail. The blacktail deer is actually a subspecies of mule deer and is found only along the west coast from Alaska to California.

Mule deer and whitetails are different both physically and behaviorally. A whitetail buck, for example, has tines that grow from the main trunk of the antler while the mule deer antler has tines that fork from the base. Mule deer have much larger ears and a white rump with a slim tail ending in a black tip. A whitetail's tail is brown on top but is much wider and when erected "flags," or shows, white. The blacktail deer looks like a cross between a mule deer and a whitetail. Its antlers fork but its tail is a narrow version of the whitetail's.

Whitetail deer range for the most part east of the Rocky Mountains and south of the boreal forest. Their range includes the southern portion of all the Canadian provinces and most of the United States except California, Alaska and Nevada.

There are several subspecies of whitetail deer ranging in size from the small Florida Key deer which weighs less than 50 pounds to northern whitetails averaging between 150 to 250 pounds for females and 200 to 400 pounds for males.

Mule deer range starts west of the Mississippi River to the Pacific coast and south from British Columbia to Mexico. Although mule deer and whitetail ranges overlap in the west, their habitats are very distinctive. Whitetails prefer woody ravines and forests while the mule deer is much more at home in the wide open spaces of the plains and high mountain slopes. The mule deer's single subspecies is the blacktail, and both weigh slightly more than the whitetail.

Mule deer are more likely to be encountered in small herds of does and fawns, especially in open rangeland, but whitetails will occasionally form small groups as well. For both species the yearly cycles are similar. Most of North America's wild deer give birth in late spring in some secluded place to their spotted fawns. Twins are common but single fawns and triplets are by no means rare. Shortly after birth the fawns are able to walk and seek nourishment from their mother. The doe has licked them dry and eaten any afterbirth to hide their scent. In the process of doing this the fawns' distinctive odor has been imprinted on her brain and she will have bonded to her babies. If, for some reason she is unable to do so in those first precious moments after birth, she will ignore her young, condemning them to a slow death. Fortunately, this rarely happens.

The fawns never bed down side by side but seek hiding places some distance apart. The doe will leave them to go off to feed and they will lie still, relying on their spotted coats and weak scent to protect them from predators. Coyotes, wolves and bears will prey on young deer and many are lost despite the doe's presence and her spirited performance to distract them from her fawns. Once the fawn is a month old, it can run and the odds for survival shift. Summer becomes a relatively safe time.

Deer are browsers and feed on the tender first-growth leaves of spring. They will graze on grass, especially early in the spring when it is the first green vegetation available to them. Summer is a lazy time when food is plentiful and the threat of predators lessens. Although bucks and does may range together in the fall and early spring, they occupy different areas of the herd's home range in summer and winter. Fawns always range with the does.

Bucks may come together in the summer, forming loosely-knit groupings to begin to establish dominance. A buck's antlers are a source of status and the bigger they are the more successful the animal is likely to be during the fall rut. Among ungulates dominant animals treat subordinates as they would females and may mount them as if mating. Dominant male and female deer will also use a foreleg kick applied to the belly or genital area to move a subordinate away from a desired food source or bed. Even this placid time of the year involves much social interaction and jockeying for status within the herd.

It is often assumed that the rut begins when the does come into heat in late fall. In fact, for the bucks it begins in early September when their antlers harden and they scrape off the velvet covering. At this time they are usually shy and hard to find, but once their antlers have hardened they are aggressive and caught up in the mating ritual. The bucks stage mock battles with resilient saplings or pine trees and rub their foreheads vigorously on the trees to mark them with their scent. They will also make "scrapes," raking the ground with their hooves until it is clear of debris and urinating on the bare ground leaving a clear signpost for other deer. Often these scrapes are further identified by a branch the buck has pulled down over it.

The final pre-mating ritual involves short pushing matches with other bucks to test their strength. By the end of summer the bucks' necks have swollen to twice their normal size to give each animal increased power for these matches. These are not the serious battles yet to come and often end with the two animals browsing peacefully beside each other.

The mating season begins about six weeks later when the first does enter estrus. The old established pecking order breaks down as new bucks follow females into another buck's range. Laid back ears and a stiff, forward walk advertise a buck's aggressive nature. Antlers serve as a measure of a buck's vigor and it is rare for a smaller-antlered buck to challenge a larger one. When two of equal size meet and neither backs down a serious battle could occur. The ferocity of such battles and the speed with which one buck is able to fend off another's parry is surprising. Deer, like other horned and antlered game, have special cones in their eyes that permit almost instantaneous reflex reactions to danger. Because of this, few battles result in any serious damage being done to either combatant. Sometimes antlers will lock and the two deer, unable to free themselves, will starve to death or fall victim to predators. On rare occasions, a buck's antler will gore its opponent, killing the deer.

The successful male will trail the doe's scent. Eventually she will accept her consort and allow mating to take place. The two will mate several times and the buck will remain with the doe for a day or so to prevent other males from breeding with her. The mating season may last until January but for most deer the rut is over by the end of December.

As winter approaches deer begin to drift to their winter range. Mule deer bucks descend from the high mountain valleys to the lower slopes where trees provide shelter and the wind blows the vegetation clear of snow. Depending on the severity of the winter some deer will "yard up." A yard, especially in the northern part of whitetail range, may consist of a large pine or spruce stand in which up to several hundred deer may gather. The animals may migrate fifty miles to such a location emptying the area of deer for miles around. The advantage of yarding is that the number of deer in the group wear down the deep snow into well-trodden paths, allowing movement while conserving energy. When wolves, coyotes or dogs get into a yard, however, the deer can be easily killed.

Deer feeding, especially in the north, has become popular for conservation clubs. Through such programs much has been learned about the herd's needs. Deer must have a good feed in December and early January if they are to survive the winter. This is especially true of the bucks who fed little during the rut. Everything is done to conserve their body reserves including the dropping of antlers which served their only real function during the rutting battles. From mid-January until the end of February the deer do little but feed and sleep in snow-packed beds while their metabolisms slow down.

The next critical time for feeding is just before fawning. Does must get food if they are to give birth to healthy young. The type of food is critical. Deer have starved to death with bellies full of corn. They must have certain bacteria in their intestines in order to break down particular foods. If a food is new to a deer's feeding habits the deer will be unable to process the food.

For both mule deer and whitetail the warming spring sun brings relief from the hazards of winter. Last year's fawns will be chased away by their mothers to fend for themselves. The does leave the herd once again to seek a quiet shelter and a new generation of life will begin. The year of the deer will have come full circle.

There is a myth that there are more deer in North America now than there ever were. This is simply not true. The arrival of the European gradually reduced the deer herd from an estimated 25 million animals to about 12 million in 1776. Later there was a slight increase in numbers as farming methods improved habitat for the deer. However, the advent of better firearms and market hunting in the mid 1800s reduced the overall herd to a few million animals and in some areas almost eliminated deer entirely. Today, thanks to modern game management the herd of whitetails numbers about 15 million animals, slightly more than half its pre-Columbian population.

While the whitetail has increased in numbers since the 1900s, the mule deer has gone through a slow but steady decline due to habitat loss. Recent awareness of this problem and modern management techniques are trying to reverse the trend, as man becomes more conscious of the need to conserve the world around him.

This mule deer fawn displays the large mule-like ears that give the species its name.

An alert whitetail deer stands
ready for flight in the snowy
forest undergrowth.

A whitetail buck loses the velvet covering from its newly matured antlers.

Whitetail deer thrive near cities and towns. River valleys, farm woodlots and parks provide good habitat.

A whitetail buck peers out from behind a stand of trees.

The raised tail of the whitetail serves as a danger warning to other deer and may even serve as a flag for fleeing deer to follow.

A whitetail doe demonstrates the grace and speed of a deer
in full flight.

The whitetail is the most common North American deer, numbering about 15 million across the continent.

A whitetail deer stands alert in a colorful field of goldenrod.

Twin mule deer fawns browse in summer grasses. The two will never bed down together but will sleep some distance apart to protect them from predators.

Immediately after birth, a new fawn will be licked clean by its mother to dispel any telltale scent. The imperceptible scent of a newborn fawn is its primary protection in the first vulnerable days.

Bucks are struck by cars most frequently during the fall
when the mating season roaming causes them to cross highways
and roadways.

Mule deer country is more open and mountainous than whitetail habitat, restricting their range to the western part of the continent.

Deer are browsers, feeding mostly on twigs and leaves although they will also eat grasses and sedges.

In these sequential photographs, a spectacular whitetail buck performs a lip curl, a mating season behavior pattern involving the stiffening of the body, a slow sideways swing of the head and a rather odd protrusion of the tongue. Often the buck appears to be bugling, although almost no vocalization occurs.

The size of a buck's antlers signals its state of health and virility to other deer.

Only bucks of equal size and strength fight.

Left: A browsing mule deer buck displays the forked antlers that are one of its distinguishing characteristics.

Above: Mule deer does frequent lower altitudes during summer grazing than their bucks.

The spotted coat of the newborn whitetail fawn serves as a camouflage until it can rely on running as a means of escaping predators.

A mature whitetail buck
stands ready to fight.

Deer mating season lasts from September to December, although in some areas it can continue into January.

An early whitetail fawn is framed by a delicate tracery of
snow-covered branches.

# ANTLERED BIG GAME

A lone caribou stands against the magnificent
backdrop of Alaska's Mount McKinley.

IT SURPRISES MANY PEOPLE TO LEARN THAT MOOSE, ELK AND caribou belong to the same family as deer. Perhaps this is because they are so much larger than deer, or because their behavior patterns are so different. Like all members of the deer family these animals have cloven hooves, chew their cud and possess antlers.

The smallest of the three species is the caribou. Found across the top of the continent, these animals range in weight from 150 to 300 pounds for females and from 275 to 600 pounds for males. Antlers on a male may be over sixty inches long and span more than four feet from tip to tip. Next in size is the elk or wapiti. A bull can weigh between 650 and 1000 pounds while the females range between 450 and 600 pounds. Their antlers can exceed five feet in length and a set may weigh over forty pounds!

Neither elk nor caribou can compare in size to the bull moose. Alaskan moose, the giants of the species, possess antlers which exceed six feet across and may weigh over seventy-five pounds. A large bull moose will top the scales at 1400 pounds while females average 900 pounds. An average bull moose will stand between six and seven feet tall at the shoulder.

While extraordinary in size, the antlers' development is typical of all antler growth. Antlers, unlike horns, are grown each year and then discarded. They are found only on males with the exception of the female caribou which grow rather small ones (twenty inches long) similar to a yearling bull's.

Antler growth begins in early spring as a reddish bud on the top of the animal's head. Beneath this bump is the "pedicle," or base, of the antler. The red color is caused by the blood bringing calcium to deposit for the antler's growth.

Light entering the eye of the animal stimulates and controls the growth by causing chemical changes in the male's metabolism. As the light increases both in hours of daylight and in quality in the spring, it causes the skin covering on the pedicle to begin formation of the ant-ler. In late summer, as the daylight hours lessen, the light signals the pituitary gland to release chemical messages that stop the antler growth and causes the male's testes to release testosterone which in turn signals the onset of the rut.

Before this happens the antlers will have grown to their full size under a layer of skin called velvet. Surprisingly, the antlers are very sensitive during this time and if bumped will bruise and cause the animal some pain. Bruises are visible in the hardened antler as unusual bumps or "drop points."

When antler growth stops, usually by the end of August, the blood ceases to bring calcium and gradually the skin covering shrinks and dries up. This causes itching and the bull begins to rub his antlers against trees to remove the annoying covering. At the same time the testosterone is causing other physical changes to happen. The neck muscles grow rapidly and the normally placid animals become aggressive and begin to seek out cows.

It is now that the true function of antlers comes into play. Once thought to be used for defense against predators, scientists now know that their main purpose is to ensure success at breeding.

Antlers are highly visible. They are red with blood at first but quickly dry to a beige or light brown color that can be seen from a distance. The size of the antler tells other members of the species about the condition of the owner. Large ones, for example, indicate that the male was successful in obtaining quality food and is in excellent health. They indicate a vigorous and virile animal, one that lesser males should avoid and that females might select as mates. Antler size and the number of points, however, are not a reliable indication of the animal's age. Only when two males of similar size meet will they engage in antler-to-antler battle.

It takes nearly as much energy to grow antlers as it does for a female to nourish a baby in her womb so once the rut is over most deer species quickly lose their antlers and begin to feed. Only the bull elk retains its antlers until the end of winter. Scientists speculate that they must be of some use against predators or other bull elk in dominance battles, but as yet this trait remains a mystery.

Socially moose, elk and caribou are quite different. Together they represent three very different strategies to ensure the success of their species.

Where an animal has evolved to live largely determines its social structure. Food is of primary importance. Animals that live on the plains have an abundance of one food source: grass. There is little competition for food and many animals may feed in the area. Hence, plains animals tend to herd, providing the protection of numbers against predators.

Forest dwellers, on the other hand, do not have an overabundance of one food resource and there is frequently some distance between stands of the preferred browse. Escaping danger in the woods is often a case of hiding in the forest or taking to the water. These needs can be achieved more effectively by a single animal.

Moose are primarily dwellers of the northern forests from Newfoundland to Alaska. Here, alone or with a calf, adult moose wander. Occasionally an abundant crop of lilies or another favorite plant will bring a few moose together but this kind of gathering does not constitute a herd.

With the coming of the fall mating season this lifestyle imposes some major obstacles, mainly how to find a mate. Moose solve the problem by making noise, lots of noise. The cow moose is the most vocal of all female deer for as she wanders she constantly calls in a long bass *moo* that can carry for a mile or more on a still day.

Bulls call, too. Their call is part warning to other bulls and part lovesong. Like other male deer they will scrape wallows and perfume themselves by urinating on their back legs and rolling in the urine-soaked ground. A night spent camped near a moose courting area is often a sleepless one, as bull and cow serenade each other from dusk to dawn.

Eventually mating occurs and the male departs. The cow will give birth in the spring to a single calf or twins, having driven off last year's offspring a few weeks before.

Caribou are dwellers of open land: the tundra. Herd size depends on the species. The woodland caribou, living year round in the boreal forest from Newfoundland to northern Alberta, for example, live in small herds. Barrenground caribou, living on the band of tundra that stretches from Labrador to Alaska, choose to live in larger herds and come together in huge herds on the calving grounds. Some of these herds number over 100,000 animals and rival the great herds of Africa. Unlike the African plains, however, the tundra is a poor environment and such herds of caribou may represent all the caribou for half a million square miles.

Caribou cows and last year's calves are the first to arrive at the calving grounds. The bulls follow along, but much later, joining the herd only after the new calves are born.

All the calves are born within a few days of each other. Grizzlies, wolves and wolverines find easy prey here and may kill 25 percent of the newborn animals. Such a slaughter could be harmful to the herds but, in fact, after a few days of feasting the predators can eat no more and the bulk of the calves survives. Had their births been spread over a month or more, the survival rate would have been much lower.

The bulls join the cows long before the rut and travel with them as they seek forage on the barrenlands. Mating begins as the herds start their long march to the shelter of the boreal forests far to the south. When the herd stops to feed, battles break out among the bulls and the herd is constantly moving as one animal chases another. Not for the caribou the bugling harem-keeping ways of the elk or the solitary, noisy honeymoon of the moose! Somehow amid all this confusion, mating occurs and the seeds of new life are planted.

Wolves following the herd find the bulls that have been chased out of the herd or have been injured easy prey. The cows, however, keep a watchful eye on behalf of the herd and any bulls inside the herd are protected by their attentiveness.

A big herd is of no advantage in the woods and the throng of animals gradually breaks up into smaller herds once in the shelter of the forest. The bulls and cows separate to seek their own range. Barren-ground caribou are creatures of the open, and even here in the forests they seek the windswept expanse of frozen northern lakes to bed, entering the forest only to feed.

Elk have adopted a lifestyle halfway between the moose and the caribou. Because they dwell in open parkland of the western states and provinces where both favored grasses and browse occur, elk can afford to live in herds. For most of the year males and females live apart, often in quite different parts of the herd's range. However, with the fall rut males begin to search out the female herds. The bulls are extremely aggressive at this time and will slash at young saplings or vent their rage by digging in the grass with their antlers. They constantly bugle their challenges, often doing so in the middle of chewing grass.

The bugle can be heard for miles as it echoes off the hills, and is one of the truly inspiring sounds of the wild. If it is high-pitched it is a young bull likely experiencing his first rut. An older bull's call is deeper, more resonant and much more impressive. It advertizes both his size and his location. If the bull has found a harem, the call tells other bulls to keep away. If he is still searching, it tells other cows that may not have found a mate where he is and they may seek him.

Finding the cows is one thing; keeping them is another. Only one female is likely to come into estrus at a time so the bull will try to keep as many in his harem as possible to ensure ample breeding opportunities. Females that are not in heat tend to wander and the bull must constantly chase after them. The more cows he controls, the more energy he wastes herding them.

A bull's constant bugling has also told rival bulls where to find females and they will move toward the herd bull's harem. If the bulls are equally matched a fight might occur. As with moose, these matches may involve a titanic struggle with each opponent slashing and pushing at the other to assert his strength. If the herd bull wins he will have the harem for a few days longer but in time the chasing and fighting will wear him out and he will give up his females to another.

If it is still early in the season the bull may yet attempt another take-over once he has regained his strength, but the process is demanding and many a big bull enters the winter drained and weakened to fall easy victim to wolves or starvation.

Each of the three different lifestyles is aimed at ensuring the success of the species. Of the three subspecies it is the moose that must be judged the most successful, for its range has expanded in the last one hundred years or so. Moose were absent from the Yellowstone and Grand Teton areas of the United States when the mountain men and trappers first came there in the early 1800s yet today these two parks provide one of the best places to see moose in North America. The north slope of Alaska's Brooks Range has only recently been colonized by moose.

Elk range has decreased. Once found on the prairies and in the eastern woodlands, the elk is now confined primarily to the Rocky Mountain parks of the west. Their numbers have been slowly increasing again, and some small range expansion has occurred in the last few decades.

Caribou have suffered the most. Modern rifles and snowmobiles have allowed hunters to take far too many caribou. The herds that once numbered several million now number less than a million across the north. Wolves in some areas, coupled with hunters, threaten the herd's regrowth and both man and predator must be controlled if the herd is to regain its former numbers.

Still for the large antlered game the outlook is brighter than for many species. The moose, elk and caribou are likely to be around for both photographers and hunters to marvel at for some time to come.

Summer elk herds consist of cows and calves.

Bull elk gather harems of females for mating season. The successful bull remains harassed by other bulls, however, and may wear itself down fighting the contenders to such an extent that it may not survive the winter.

A bull elk in summer velvet.

72

Moose are solitary creatures, seeking each other out only during mating season.

These three bull moose have been brought together only by the lush feeding in the river and will soon separate.

At their seasonal peak, bull moose antlers may weigh seventy-five pounds and span six feet.

Left: The magnificent antlers of the bull elk, like all deer species, are shed each year and grown anew.

Above: A bull elk grazes in solitary splendor.

Calf elk are spotted for protection like other deer.

A bull moose browses on almost out-of-reach branches.

A woodland caribou displays a breathtaking set of antlers.

Elk lock antlers in combat. Although dominance is usually established without injury, an elk will occasionally be gored by his opponent.

A young bull moose's antlers
are covered with soft summer
velvet.

Light entering the eye has stimulated and controlled the growth of this elk's antlers. As the sunlight grows in strength and duration each year, the animal's metabolism is triggered to produce the season's antlers.

Two pairs of barrenground caribou lock antlers in battle to determine dominance. Occasionally, the caribou cannot unlock their antlers and are doomed to a slow death.

A massive bull moose displays
the extraordinary profile
characteristic of this ungainly
yet spectacular animal.

Moose are excellent swimmers and will even dive to shallow lake bottoms for food.

# HORNED GAME

Desert bighorn sheep of the western desert region have come back from the brink of extinction but are still endangered.

THE HORNED ANIMALS OF NORTH AMERICA REPRESENT THE BEST and the worst of man's relationship with wildlife. Among their stories are tales of near extinction, incredible revivals, compounded stupidity and impending failures. That this should be so is perhaps due to the horns these animals possess.

Horns grow on a bony core forming a hard covering about it. Horns removed from the core are hollow and resemble a knife's sheath. The horn material itself is much the same as that found in fingernails only thicker. Horns, with the exception of those of the pronghorns, add a layer each year and can be used to age the animal in much the same way a tree's growth rings can tell how old a tree is.

Horns, unlike antlers, do not fall off each year. Instead they continue to grow, becoming larger and more valued by hunters as trophies. Horned animals have also been the ones domesticated by man and include sheep, goats and cattle. Settlers arriving on the plains found the wild relatives of their stock pleasant and ample food substitutes. Some horned animals, like the bison, were too large and numerous to be tolerated by an agricultural society and were decimated to make room for the plow and the ranch.

North America's horned animals include, besides the bison, bighorn and Dall's sheep, pronghorn antelope, mountain goat and muskox. Each has a conservation story to tell.

The story of the buffalo or bison is perhaps the best-known. Once the great plains of the central region of the North American continent were home to an estimated 25 to 60 million of these animals. They were found from the Atlantic to the Pacific coasts but the bison east of the Mississippi, never plentiful, were gone by the beginning of the 1800s. It wasn't until the westward expansion of the 1830s that the incredible numbers of these animals became known.

At first they were only an annoyance to pioneers in a hurry to get to the coast but, as the great plains were seen to be potential ranchland and farmland, the bison clearly had to go. They competed with cattle for grass; they were too big and numerous to handle easily; their hides made good leather and their meat was tasty. Politically they were seen as a way to end the "Indian threat" to settlement for the bison meant life itself to the plains Indian, supplying food, shelter, weapons and clothing. So the vast herds were hunted to the brink of extinction.

Far-sighted individuals collected some of the survivors and these eventually were returned to national, state and provincial parks. Today Yellowstone National Park's bison herd is the largest and only free-roaming herd south of Canada. Here, in places like Hayden Valley, it is possible to see almost a thousand head of animals grazing on the high plain.

Canada's Wood Buffalo National Park is home to the world's largest free-roaming herd which fluctuates between 5,000 and 15,000 animals. These animals, like Yellowstone's, are hybrids of two species: the plains and the wood, or mountain, bison. When the smaller plains bison were re-introduced into these parks, they bred with the few remaining wood bison, producing a mixture with characteristics more closely resembling the plains bison. This nearly cost the world the wood bison.

Fortunately a small "pure" herd of the darker and larger wood bison was found in a Canadian park and a number were taken to other parks and zoos where they were bred to keep the species alive. Plans now call for the release of a new wild herd of these bison, bred from zoo stock, on the Ontario-Manitoba border.

The plains bison is doing very well in other parks where it has been kept as a "pure" species. Some ranchers have found that they can be kept as cattle on the northern range where they require less care than cows. The future of this subspecies seems secure as well.

The pronghorn antelope's history parallels the bison's. Overhunting and range depletion caused its numbers to drop from over 20 million to less than 20,000. By the early 1900s conservation efforts were being made to save this species from oblivion. The pronghorn is not a true antelope. It is the only member of its prehistoric family now living and is found only in North America. As well, it has the distinction of being the only "horned" mammal to lose its horns every year. The horny covering grows back each time over a slightly larger core. Like most open-country animals pronghorn antelope live in herds. They rely on eyesight and speed to protect them from predators.

Cattlemen at first wanted them removed from the range because it was thought that they competed with cattle for grass. When it became known that pronghorn were browsers feeding especially on sage brush, which cattle will not eat, many ranchers welcomed the deer-like animals to their lands. Today it is not uncommon to see pronghorn and cattle grazing side-by-side. Thanks to government and private efforts there are now close to half a million pronghorn antelope in North America, making it second only to deer as the continent's most populous game animal.

Muskox were completely eliminated from the United States by the 1890s. Prehistoric survivors from the ice age, they were ill-equipped to cope with modern guns. Muskox are best-known for their habit of forming a circle around their offspring to protect them against wolves or Inuit hunters. The technique had some advantages, for muskox have a very thick "boss" where the base of their horns meet on the forehead. This coupled with their thick, woolly coats gave them ample protection against everything but a bullet.

In 1936 a herd of thirty-four animals imported from Greenland was released on Nunivak Island off the western coast of Alaska. Today they number over 1000 and have since been used to start other wild herds in the state. Canadian herds number about 15,000 animals while the Greenland herd remains stable at about 10,000. Although few in number these relics of a time when woolly rhinos and mammoths wandered the north seem to face a secure future.

Mountain goats represent the disadvantage of introducing a species into a new environment. Like the pronghorn and the muskox, the white goat of the mountains was a survivor of ice age fauna. Of all the big game species, this animal fared the best, for it chose as its range the highest peaks of the Rocky Mountains and the coastal mountains.

Even in the bleakest days of winter, these animals clung to the cliffs waiting out the storm, seldom venturing into the protection of the forest below. Few hunters bothered with them and, while not abundant, the goat population was stable.

Seeking to expand its range, conservation-minded people transported some goats to new territories, notably Olympic National Park in Washington state and the Black Hills of South Dakota on Hearney Peak and Mount Rushmore. The Black Hills transplant did well. The goats thrived without doing much harm to their environment. The Olympic population on the other hand was too successful. The goat population filled the new territory and prospered in the mountains nourished by moist breezes from the Pacific Ocean. They found many of the plants there to their liking and it soon became apparent that these new residents might threaten the survival of several native plants. The problem facing biologists today is how to control or remove the goats without a storm of protest from the public.

Most of the horned animals have been conservation success stories. Sadly, this is not so for the wild sheep. North America's wild sheep are spectacular animals inhabiting the mountains from Alaska and the Yukon south to Mexico. There are two types: the bighorn and the thin horn species.

The bighorn group is generally divided into two subspecies: Rocky Mountain bighorn sheep and the desert bighorn. These animals have horns with thick bases that curl around and inward. The Rocky Mountain animals are the biggest of their kind and the best-known. In parks, like Canada's Banff and Jasper, tourists frequently see them by the roadside seeking salt at natural licks along the highway. This view of the sheep in high mountain pastures presents an inaccurate picture of the animals, for they were once more common in the grasslands adjacent to the west's badlands and in steep river valleys. Here they were very vulnerable to hunting pressure, and subspecies like Audubon's bighorn became extinct before 1900. Only in their mountain strongholds have the sheep held out in any numbers. Sadly, even here disease and poaching are reducing the herd and its future, despite transplants and increased protection, may not be guaranteed.

The desert bighorn have come back from the brink of extinction but they too are not out of danger. They are thinner and rangier than their northern cousins and eke out an existence in poor desert terrain. That they have survived the release of feral mules which compete for grasses, as well as man's guns, is a tribute to some well-thought-out conservation planning but their future is not secure.

The thin horned sheep arrived in North America much more recently than did their bigger cousins. Like all the horned animals, with the exception of the pronghorn, they arrived from Asia across the land bridge created by the ice age. That same ice prevented them from migrating further south and confined them to central Alaska. When it melted they moved into new territories but never ventured as far south as the bighorn range.

Their horns curl outward and are much thinner than their southern cousins'. There are two subspecies: the all-white Dall's sheep of Alaska and the Yukon and the darker Fannin or stone sheep of northern British Columbia. Both have relatively stable populations; their numbers are not great but they are doing better than the bighorn populations.

All the horned animals have similar habits. All are herd animals in which, for most of the year, the males live in separate herds. An exception is the pronghorn which will generally stay with the females when it is not rutting season.

When the rut begins all male members of the horned species clash heads in ritualized battle to determine dominance. Mountain goat battles are by far the most dangerous for the animals because they are fought on precarious footing and because the dagger-like horns can inflict severe injury.

Despite similarities each species has its own distinctive needs and characteristics. In some cases man's relationship with them has not impeded their survival. In others, man's interference has created new problems for them and for us. Current agricultural and other land uses will never allow these horned animals the luxury of returning to their pre-Columbian numbers. That is something that naturalists, hunters and ranchers have come to regard as acceptable. However, all agree that while numbers must be limited, the loss of any of these species in a wild state is catastrophic. With some luck and good management horned game should remain a part of North America's rich wildlife heritage.

The range of the Rocky Mountain bighorn was once much broader than it is today, and could be found along river valleys and into the prairie badlands. Except for a few introduced populations they are now strictly confined to their mountain ranges.

The pronghorn antelope is not a true antelope. It is the only
surviving member of its prehistoric family and is found only in
North America.

Pure wood bison such as these now exist only in captive herds. Scientists hope to reintroduce herds into the wild within the next few years.

A bighorn ewe and her lamb traverse the snow-covered mountainous terrain of the Columbia Icefields in Canada.

Tongue protruding, a bull bison bellows his warning to rival bulls.

A racing calf muskox shows the guard hairs of its winter coat. This outer coat traps air for insulation against the harsh arctic winters.

Mountain goats spend most of their lives above the treeline and
seldom leave their home range.

A herd of mountain goats ambles comfortably over a precariously rocky cliff-face.

Left: The size of a bighorn ram's horns determines its status. Unlike antlers, horns are not shed but grow larger every year.

Above: A bighorn ewe and her lamb show how skilfully their coat coloration blends in with their habitat. At any distance, these two would be impossible to see.

This bighorn ram displays an impressive set of horns and has started to "broom" them, rubbing down the tips so that they don't impede his vision.

The pronghorn is the fastest mammal in North America and can exceed speeds of sixty miles per hour.

Two Dall's rams crash on an Alaskan slope. All horned and antlered game fight head-to-head.

A bighorn ewe perches above a breathtaking alpine lake.

Wild sheep are grazers, sometimes foraging on the same ground as domestic sheep and cattle. Sharing winter range increases the exposure of each species to the other's diseases.

Overhunting and range depletion caused the pronghorn's numbers to drop from over 20 million to less than 20,000 by the nineteenth century. Conservation efforts in our century have brought the pronghorn back from the brink of extinction.

The bull bison (top) and the muskox (bottom) each perform a lip curl or flehem during mating season to indicate that they have found a female in heat. All ungulates share this odd behavior.

A flock of Dall's ewes and lambs grazes on a mountain slope.

Like the pronghorn and the muskox, the mountain goat is a
survivor of the ice age.

# SMALL GAME: PREDATORS AND PREY

The lynx, a beautiful wildcat of the northern woodlands, feeds mainly upon snowshoe hare. Its population fluctuates according to the numbers of the hare, an example of the complex and delicate balance of the world's ecosystems.

OUTNUMBERING THE BIG GAME ANIMALS BY A WIDE MARGIN IS A group of animals classified under the broad heading of small game. This group is composed of rabbits, groundhogs, squirrels, prairie dogs, foxes, wolves and "cats," a surprising collection of both predators and prey.

The role of predators in the ecosystem is often a controversial one. Man has made war on them, even hunting them in national parks. The hatred of wolves and mountain lions, or cougars, probably stemmed from the fact that both man and wild predators preyed on the same species. Wolf and coyote were viewed as competition for deer and elk. They were also seen as a threat to ranch stock and were shot to keep cattle and sheep safe.

The attempted removal of predators from many of North America's parks, shows the misguided attitude of wildlife managers in the early years of this century. Research begun in the 1930s has given us a much more realistic picture of the needs of game animals, small and large, predator and prey. Killers of livestock cannot be tolerated but now conservation officers seek to remove only the offending animals from the area, not all members of the species. In parts of Canada and the northern United States where rabies is prevalent, this approach has produced an unexpected benefit.

Coyotes are most often the major wild predator on sheep and so are hated by farmers. It was discovered, however, that if only the sheep-killing coyotes were taken (not an easy task), leaving other coyotes in the area, it tended to restrict the number of red foxes. Foxes carry rabies but coyotes seldom do. By tolerating coyotes (which will eat a red fox given the chance), the incidence of rabies, that cattle, sheep and man alike can contract, was reduced.

Unfortunately such understanding of the complexity of nature's balance came too late for the wolf. Throughout the entire continental United States the wolf is either extinct or exists in small, isolated pockets such as in Yellowstone and Isle Royale national parks. Only in Canada and Alaska has the wolf survived the hunting and trapping pressure applied to it. Indeed, only recently has it achieved status as a game animal. This status means that wolf numbers will be managed to keep the population healthy but in check. Most biologists now feel that wolves provide a valuable service to their prey species by removing sick or injured animals although they also take a number of young and old animals and very occasionally even a healthy adult.

Many scientists now believe that there are times when man must severely limit wolf numbers for the good of the prey species. This usually occurs where both man and wolf are hunting the same species. Man can limit his season and kill but the wolf hunts and kills all year. No biologist, however, advocates killing off all the wolves.

Wolf numbers also appear to be controlled by some of their prey. Moose have reduced wolf numbers in shared habitat, to the great surprise of scientists studying their interrelationship.

In Isle Royale National Park of the United States, for example, the moose population exceeded its winter range and began starving. The wolves, finding easy pickings, increased in numbers to fifty animals, about three times their normal density. The moose population plummeted from about 1200 animals to 600 and it was feared that pressure from the large wolf packs on those few remaining animals would eliminate moose from the island. A surprising thing happened. The moose now had plenty of food and were very healthy. When the wolves attacked the moose stood their ground and fought off the wolves. Deprived of their prey the wolves began fighting and killing each other and the wolf population plummeted too, bringing the two species back into balance.

The wolves of Algonquin Park of Ontario, on the other hand, faced a different problem. For years Algonquin had few moose and large numbers of whitetail deer because the deer carried a brain worm which did not affect them but which killed moose. As long as Algonquin was good deer country the moose were a rarity and the wolves fed on the deer herd. However, with improved forestry management techniques the logged-over park changed and the forest canopy grew too high for deer, shifting the environment in favor of the moose. The deer died out and the moose came back with a vengeance. In the 1960s there were about 600 moose in the park. Today they exceed 3000 animals! Algonquin's wolves were ill-equipped to cope with this change. They had no idea how to hunt moose and their numbers dropped. They have still to recover and those that survived did so by eating beaver and smaller game.

One type of wolf, the coyote, has thrived despite an all-out attempt to control its numbers. It has been hunted from airplanes, snowmobiles and with dogs. It has been poisoned, trapped and even dynamited and yet, more than any other North American species, it has increased its range, replacing the gray wolf in the east, the north and the west.

Coyotes now live on the border of virtually every major city on the continent and in almost every state and province. For the most part the species survives by eating mice, small birds and rabbits. It can take deer but does so rarely. It does, unfortunately, occasionally feed on sheep and cattle.

Another large predator that appears to be expanding its range is the cougar. The western subspecies is moving east and there is plenty of indication that the eastern and Florida subspecies may not have become extinct as was believed a few years ago. The resurgence of this large cat seems to be linked to the growing population of whitetail deer throughout its range. Cougars are never common and the true status of this animal in the north and southeast remains an unanswered question.

Bobcat numbers seem to be declining throughout their mid-continent range. This is due more to overtrapping than to hunting pressure although the bobcat is taken as both a game animal and a furbearer. Recent attempts have been made to breed the animals on ranches and might prove beneficial for the wild populations by removing pressure from them.

Lynx, too, are being bred in captivity. New management techniques survey wild lynx trappers and when the population undergoes its cyclic crash every five to seven years, all trapping of the long-legged cat ceases for two or more years. Captive breeding ranches might be able to supply the demand during these low periods and reduce the risk of losing wild lynx to poachers.

The story behind the lynx population cycle is a good illustration of nature's complex balance. Lynx feed on the snowshoe hare, and it was once thought that the two animals controlled each other's numbers. When lynx numbers were low this allowed more young hares to survive, increasing the snowshoe population. Lynx, with more hare to hunt, had a better year and more of their young survived until finally, it was reasoned, there were too many lynx eating too many rabbits and the snowshoe population crashed.

We now know it was not the lynx that caused the crash of the snowshoe hare but the plants on which they fed. When the rabbit population was low they did little damage to the few types of plants they fed on but, as the hare numbers increased, they threatened the very survival of these plants. To counteract this the plants undergo a chemical change which lowers their nutritional value. Poorer food affects the female's reproductive tract and few hares are born the next year. The population crashes and the following year, deprived of their prime food source, so do lynx numbers.

Man's relationship with non-predatory game animals has had two aspects to it. They were treated as food — cottontails, jackrabbits and squirrels — or as vermin — marmots, groundsquirrels and prairie dogs.

Small food game has fared better because a hunting season controlled the kill. Vermin, on the other hand, were destroyed because they caused damage to livestock. Farmers and ranchers believed that cattle or horses running through a prairie dog town in the west or through a groundhog colony in the east could break a leg in one of the many holes. This is, in fact, an extremely rare occurrence and the prejudice against these animals is largely unfounded.

To wander through a prairie dog town in one of the national or state parks in the Dakota states is to experience an incredible diversity of life in a small area. Coyotes prowl in the morning and evening, burrowing owls peer out of vacated prairie dog holes, and rattlers and badgers hunt there regularly. Overhead a golden eagle may fly by in search of easy prey. Bull bison wallow in the soft earth around the entrances, stirring up dust to advertise their presence to females and pronghorns regularly pass through as they search for browse.

Watchers of such towns have discovered that the "town" consists of small clusters of related sisters — females of litters who regularly "kiss" nose to nose to verify their relationship. Should a strange "dog" enter, it is quickly evicted.

Groundhogs, among the least social of the marmots and squirrels, have a less structured society designed to keep the families evenly spaced. Their Rocky Mountain cousins, the hoary and yellowbellied marmots, are more social and will play together as youngsters. Any hiker in the west has heard their shrill whistles warning others of the hiker's approach.

Whether viewed through a camera lens or binoculars, or stalked with a rifle, these animals along with the other game animals of North America provide hours of recreational pleasure for many people. They are also a part of a balanced and healthy ecosystem. It has been said that as long as there are grizzlies and wolves, the ecosystem is healthy. Remove even one of the smaller game species, or even non-game animals, and the future of all predators, including man, is placed in jeopardy.

A hoary marmot nestles amid the bright flowers of an alpine meadow.

The cottontail rabbit ranges over all of North America, and is a
common sight in fields and meadows.

There are several species of groundsquirrel in the west. This one, the Columbian groundsquirrel, is found at lower altitudes in the northern Rocky Mountains.

Its cousin, the arctic groundsquirrel, shown here, is also known as the parka squirrel because the Inuit use its fur to line their parkas.

The bobcat is a smaller relative of the lynx. Overhunting and trapping have depleted its numbers but it is still found throughout much of its original mid-continent range.

The cougar, or mountain lion, is North America's most spectacular big cat. Once concerned that the cougar was becoming endangered, scientists now note that it appears to be expanding eastward out of its western range and that the eastern cougar, presumed extinct, has reappeared in northeastern Canada.

The hoary marmot lives in the high alpine meadows of the western
mountains. It may hibernate for up to eight months of the year.

The desert cottontail has larger ears than temperate climate cottontails to allow its body heat to radiate from their surfaces. Like most desert animals, it also tends to be smaller than its relatives.

A yellow-bellied marmot peers cautiously from its rocky ledge. These marmots range over much of the west from southern Canada to New Mexico.

The red fox, like other foxes, is actually a member of the dog family. Unlike other members of the dog family that hunt by running down their prey, foxes stalk and pounce like cats.

Coyotes are also known as prairie or brush wolves. Their traditional range covers the deserts, prairie, open woodlands and brush country of the west, although they have adapted to survival at the edges of cities and seem to be expanding eastward.

The groundhog, or woodchuck, is the eastern relative of the marmot. Of all the marmots, it is the least social, preferring to live apart from other members of its species.

Superstition holds that if a groundhog awakens from its winter hibernation on February 2, and sees its shadow, there will be six more weeks of winter.

A bobcat peers out from a rock crevice in which it has been napping. Bobcat are primarily nocturnal animals and will seek the safety of rocky ledges or brush cover to sleep away the day.

A bobcat kitten lies ready to pounce in mock attack should a leaf flutter in front of its nose, or an unsuspecting fly buzz into range.

Once the black, or gray, squirrel numbered in the millions across the unbroken forests of the east but as the forest was cut down, their numbers plummeted. Today this familiar and still abundant squirrel lives in numbers that only hint at its previous population.

The red squirrel is a smaller relative of the black. Like all squirrels, its broad, bushy tail acts as a rudder when the animal leaps and as a parachute when it drops.

Raccoons are clever, adaptable animals that have learned to thrive within urban environments. They are a common sight now in many northeastern cities of North America.

The wolf has entered the western imagination as a symbol of stealth and hunting skill and cleverness. Research has shown that these magnificent animals, although all these things and more, do not deserve the hate and fear with which man has faced them.

A wolf, when cornered, will lay back its ears, crouch and growl just as a dog does, but will only attack if it feels it is its only recourse for survival.

Cougars, also known as pumas, are shy, solitary creatures that avoid contact with humans. They can be as much as seven feet long, including their thirty-inch tail, and can weigh up to 175 pounds.

A lynx feeds on the remains of a deer. Although lynx survive
primarily on the snowshoe hare, they may occasionally take
larger prey.

A coyote peers into the distance, keeping a watchful eye for any movement that could indicate possible prey.

Wolves maintain an intense family bond. Although only the
dominant male and female of the pack mate, all members will look
after the young.

In the nineteenth century, a single prairie dog town could have several million inhabitants. A steady campaign by farmers and ranchers to exterminate them has reduced them to small pockets of their original range.

A European hare peers cautiously above its hiding place in the tall grass. Introduced into eastern North America in the nineteenth century, it is also incorrectly known as a jackrabbit. True jackrabbits are found only in the west.

A cottontail hopes it isn't noticed amid the tall grasses and
fallen leaves.

Two cougars lounge warily on a rock ledge. North American cougars are the same species as those found in the mountainous regions of South America where they are most commonly known as pumas.

A pert red fox displays the trim black legs and magnificent
red-and-white coat for which it is famous.

A Columbian groundsquirrel
feeds on a nut amid lush
summer greenery.

Two black-tailed prairie dogs look out at the world from the
safety of their doorway. Prairie dogs are named for their sharp,
barking cry.

A coyote's coat blends perfectly with the timber bark behind it.

Lord of the forest, a magnificent white-phase timber wolf stands against the autumn colors.

# PHOTO INDEX

Antelope, pronghorn, 92, 100 (bottom), 104

Bear,
  black, 18, 19 (bottom), 24, 25, 26, 27, 30, 32
  grizzly, 20, 21, 22, 23, 26 (top), 31, 33
  Kermode's black, 19 (top)
  polar, 10, 26 (bottom), 28, 29
bison, 93, 95 (top), 105 (top)
bobcat, 118, 126, 127
brush wolf. *See* coyote
buffalo. *See* bison

Caribou, 2, 62, 77 (bottom), 81
cougar, 7, 119, 132, 138
coyote, 9, 123, 134, 142

Deer,
  mule, 40, 48, 50, 51, 56, 57
  whitetail, 34, 41, 42, 43, 44, 45, 46, 49, 52–53, 54, 55, 58, 59, 60, 61

Elk, 69, 70, 71, 74, 75, 76, 78, 80

Fox, red, 122, 139

Goat, mountain, 96, 97, 107
groundhog, 124, 125

groundsquirrel,
  arctic, 117
  Columbia, 116, 140

Hare, European, 136 (bottom)

Lynx, 108, 133

Marmot,
  hoary, 114, 120
  yellow-bellied, 121 (bottom)
moose, 72, 73, 77 (top), 79, 82, 83
mountain lion. *See* cougar
muskox, 95 (bottom), 105 (bottom)

Prairie dog, 136 (top)
  black-tailed, 141
puma. *See* cougar

Raccoon, 129

Sheep,
  bighorn, 91, 94, 98, 99, 100 (top), 102, 103
  Dall's, 1, 101, 106
  desert bighorn, 84
squirrel,
  black, 128 (top)
  red, 128 (bottom)

Wapiti. *See* elk
wolf, timber, 130, 131, 135, 143